T0149311

MY GIFT TO THE WORLD

Anonymous

WESTBOW
PRESS®
A DIVISION OF THOMAS NELSON
& ZONDERVAN

Scripture quotations marked (KJV) are from the King James Version.

WestBow Press books may be ordered through booksellers or by contacting:

WestBow Press
A Division of Thomas Nelson & Zondervan
1663 Liberty Drive
Bloomington, IN 47403
www.westbowpress.com
1 (866) 928-1240

ISBN: 978-1-5127-7541-9 (sc)
ISBN: 978-1-5127-7543-3 (hc)
ISBN: 978-1-5127-7542-6 (e)

Library of Congress Control Number: 2017902175

Print information available on the last page.

WestBow Press rev. date: 3/3/2017

TABLE OF CONTENTS

INTRODUCTION

Many people have told me when I share with them these poems that Father Yahweh has given me to write that I am gifted and that I need to get a book published. As I was thinking of the title for this book Father Yahweh laid on my heart to call it, "MY GIFT TO THE WORLD," because many people have told me that I am gifted in writing poetry but when I shared the title with some of my friends they said that it sounded kind of boastful but that is the title that Father Yahweh gave me and so therefore the book is anonymous. None of the words that are in these poems are mine. Every single word that is in these poems have already been spoken by everyone before and so it is the order of the words that is different. Father Yahweh gave me the words to write in the order that they're in and it is His Name and Yeshua's Name, (also known as Jesus,) that needs to be spread throughout the world and Glorified! Not Mine!

(Some words in these poems are capitalized that normally wouldn't be but the reason they are is I'm just stressing its importance!)

NOTE OF ENCOURAGEMENT

For a long time I had been looking and praying for someone to help me with the illustration for the cover of this book and then one day something happened that sent me to a medical clinic.

One morning when I woke up I heard the name Julie in my heart. I felt like Father Yahweh was wanting me to pray for a Julie and so I did.

That day at work, I worked in construction, I was helping a co-worker carry a 50lb form. It had snowed there a little the day before but there wasn't any snow on the ground that day but there was a little bit of ice on the ground that I did not see. When carrying my side of the form I slipped on some ice and I pulled my left hand out from under the form but I didn't pull my right hand out in time and so when my hand landed on the ground, the form landed on my hand and my hand was very much swollen within a second. My superintendent took me to a medical clinic and the doctor came in to see me. He looked at my hand and he said, "I will send someone to take you to get an ex-ray. A few minutes later a lady walked in and said, "Hi. My Name is Julie. I'm going to take you to get an ex-ray." As I followed her back to the ex-ray room I was thinking, "I heard the name Julie in my heart this morning." I shared with Julie what happened that morning and I shared with her a couple of poems and guess what my friends? Julie is the one whom Father Yahweh used to draw the illustration for the cover of this book and so remember this, ""When something that seems bad happens don't always think of it as such because it may just be Father Yahweh at work."" Sometimes, if not many times, we must go through, "Something like this," to meet the person/persons and/or get to the place that is in The Father's Plans for our life!"" That morning I prayed and said, "Father Yahweh, whatever happens today is in Your Hands," and then I broke my thumb and then I met the person, who's name I heard in my heart that morning, who would draw the illustration for the cover of this book! BE ENCOURAGED!!!

A POEM ALREADY WRITTEN

These poems that I write were already written
Long before I wrote them down
For the words came to me from Heaven
Gently and without a sound

For Father Yahweh had laid them on my heart as I was searching
And I was asking Him what I should write
And because I was seeking and going by faith
Then I saw the words without using my sight

For as I lay the pen upon the paper
The ink just started to flow
And my hand just started to move
I didn't know which way to go

For The Love of Father Yahweh was moving my hand
And the pen never run dry
And the words that I was writing I knew were special
For they came to me down from the sky

And so these poems that I write, they were already written
They were first wrote up in Heaven Above
And because I was seeking and searching what to write
Then Father Yahweh moved my hand with His Love

And so these poems that I write, they're not mine
I am just a person who wrote them down
For the words came to me from Heaven
Gently and without a sound

A LETTER FROM FATHER YAHWEH

I am writing this poem from experience
I have held a pen many times
I have pulled out many sheets of paper
And I have written several rhymes

A lot of the rhymes were hard
Because it was something I tried to do all by myself
But then when I got tired of trying
I just threw the paper back upon the shelf

Then other times the rhymes weren't hard
Because I let The Love of Father Yahweh move my hand
And the ink just fell from the pen
And it was written in a way that you and I could understand

But don't give me any of the credit
Just give it all to our Father Up Above
For I just held the pen
And He moved my hand with His Love

THE GREATEST POEM EVER WRITTEN

The greatest poem that has ever been written
Is a poem that has never been heard
It is a poem not written on paper
Nor described with inexpressible words

It is a poem that does not have an ending
But it must have a special place where it starts
For it is a poem with a very special meaning
Because it is written within your heart

The greatest poem that has ever been written
Was when a person's voice was heard without them making a sound
When their voice was lifted up way above the sky
And they helped everybody to see the beauty that was all around

Their actions went to work as people stood by
And a very important message was heard
But the funny thing is the person who was talking
Never did say a word

And so the greatest poem, I think, that will ever be written
It doesn't necessarily need to rhyme
Because the greatest poem, that I think, will ever be written
Will be written between your heart and mine

THE MESSAGE

Forever is a long time
To some it may seem
But for me it is as long as something may last
It is almost like a dream

For a dream does not last forever
For all dreams do come to an end
But the outcome of your dream will last forever
Because it is a message that you will send

It is a message sent by your own life
In which you live every single day
It is a message brought forth by the light in your eyes
And the character in which you play

For the whole world it seems is like a stage
And we all play our own different part
And we are passing a baton to the next runner up
In a race that we don't have to start

For this race that we run had already been started
By our forefathers long ago
And they were trying to send a message for the whole world to hear
So together we would know

"That the character in which we choose to play
Will be the message that we will send
And the message that we bring forth
Will last from now until the end!"

THE POWER OF WORDS

Words are very powerful
They can cut like a knife
They can either destroy
Or give life

So please be careful
With the words that you use
And I hope that no one
Is ever confused

Confused by thinking
That I am such a smart guy
Because the words that I write
They come down from the sky

For I pray and I ask Yeshua
To give me the words that I should use
And now anyone who reads what I write
Should never be confused

For these poems belong to Yeshua
He just gave them to me to write down
And like one poem that I wrote says
He gave them to me gently and without a sound

And so I must be very careful
With the words that I use
Because if I don't speak the words in the order Yeshua gives me
Then many who read what I write may be confused

But it's not just me
But you must be careful with what you say
You must speak what is right
Every single day

For the words that we speak are very powerful
And they can cut deep, just like a knife
They can either destroy
Or give life

A POEM INSIDE EACH OF US

There is a poem inside each of us that is waiting to be written
For there is a message in each poem that needs to be heard
It is a message that needs to travel from person to person
And to fly through the air like a bird

It is a message that only you can write
It is a message that only you can send
It is a message that is inside of you
And it is a message that will never end

For no one else can reach the world the way you can
No one else has your dream
No one else has your vision
And no one else knows what your life means

But others will watch how you live
And you can effect eternity until the end
You just never know where your influence will stop
So be careful with how you live your life my friend

Because the poem that is inside of you can only be written
If you live your life for Yeshua every single day
And the message in your poem can only be heard
If it is written the right way

It has to be written with lives that are crazy about Yeshua
For Those Poems are The True Poems that are waiting to be heard
And These Poems are Examples in how we should live
And These Poems will fly through the air like a bird

And so there is A True Poem inside each of us that is waiting to be written
But It can only be written if you live your life for Yeshua everyday
For These are The Only True Poems and the other stuff is rap
And that is all that I have to say

THE COURAGE TO LIVE A DREAM

The courage to live a dream
Is like walking on the moon
It is like taking a leap of faith
Not really knowing just what to do

Not really knowing just where you will end up
But yet you believe with all of your heart
That where ever the road leads you will follow
And you will make a brand new start

You will make a new beginning
In this life that you live
And you will learn that the best things come
To those who are willing to give

To those who are willing to sacrifice
And to die for what they believe
For if you believe then you must pay a price
But at the end you will achieve

You will achieve the goal you were reaching
And you will have earned the right to live
For you died for what you believed in
And from your life you did give

You gave an Important Message,(The Bible!)
For all the world to hear
Your voice was heard without you making a noise
Because your actions were very clear

Your actions helped to demonstrate
What it means to live a dream
And it helped to show that in times of darkness
There is always a Huge Beam,(Yeshua!)

There is always a Huge Beam of Light, (Yeshua!)
To guide you safely to the door
And if you follow The Light and you walk through
Then you will accomplish so much more

And then the day will come when all is completed
For you will have done all that you needed to do
For you had courage and you showed what it takes
For anyone to make it through

THE BEST MESSAGE EVER PREACHED

What can I write that has never been written
What can I teach that has never been taught
What can I say that has never been spoken
And what can I buy that has never been bought

What is my life that I should live it
What good in my life have I ever done
And if my life lived is not lived for Yeshua
Then does my life have any meaning under the sun

For I am just a creature and Yeshua is The Creator
He created me to give Glory unto Him
He created me to help others
And He created me to be your friend

And for the reason that He created me
He created you for the same reason too
He created you to help others
No matter what they do unto you

For it only takes one person
To start doing what is right
And then everyone else will start to follow in
Because they saw the message just by using their sight

And so preach the best message that you can
And if you have to use words
For most often the best message preached is one that is lived
And not necessarily heard

THE RIPPLE EFFECT

When you throw a stone in the middle of a lake
The ripples from around the stone clearly show
That things do happen from actions taking place
Because there for a minute the water had a different flow

There may have been a duck floating on the water
Or a fish swimming in the sea
But when the stone was thrown and landed in the water
A ripple effect was created by either you or me

And so now for a minute think of your life
As a stone being thrown in the middle of a lake
And imagine what happens to everything around you
Because of the actions that you decided to take

Did the impact of your actions scare a duck or a fish
Did you hurt someone that you do or do not know
And did the ripple effect from your actions cause that person to hurt
someone else
Well that is an answer that you may never know

And so remember, every word that you say
And every action that you take
It creates a ripple effect
Just like throwing a stone in the middle of a lake

Because your actions and your words, they will affect eternity
You just never know where your influence will end
So live your life for Father Yahweh every single day
And let Father Yahweh's Message be The Message you send

MY LIFE LIVED

If my life lived is able to reach out
And touch 1 person's life for the good
Then my life lived has served its purpose
Because it was lived the way that it should

If my life lived is able to reach out
And touch 2 people's lives for the good
Then my life lived has served its purpose
Because it was lived the way that it should

And if my life lived is able to reach out
And touch the whole wide world for the good
Then my life lived has served its purpose
Because it was lived the way that it should

But if my life lived never reaches out
And touches anyone's life for the good
Then my life lived never served its purpose
Because it wasn't lived the way that it should

So whether I just touch 1 person's life or the whole wide world
Or any number in between
Then I will have learned a valuable lesson
And I will have learned what life really means

So whether it's just 1 person's life or the whole wide world
Or any number between the two
Then my life lived has definitely served its purpose
Because I did what I was created to do

REPLANTED WITH LOVE

A few months ago Aunty Fe asked me to pull the weeds in the back yard. As I was pulling the weeds I saw something that appeared to be a weed but I wasn't quite sure. Aunty Fe wasn't home and so I went in and asked Uncle Tony to come out and tell me if that was a weed or not. He came out and saw it and said, "Go ahead and pull it. That's a weed," and so I pulled it out of the ground and threw it in the trash with all of the other weeds.

A few hours later Aunty Fe came home and asked me where the okra plant was. I said, "What okra plant?" She showed me where it was before I pulled it out of the ground and I told her I was unsure if it was a weed or not and so I asked Uncle Tony and he said it was a weed and so I pulled it out of the ground and threw it in the trash with all of the other weeds. I could tell that Aunty Fe was a little sad and so I looked in the trash can and the okra plant was on the very top. After just a few hours of being in the trash can the okra plant looked withered away, it looked lifeless, and it looked hopeless. I told Aunty Fe that the okra plant was in the trash can and that maybe she could replant it. Aunty Fe replanted this withered away, lifeless, and hopeless looking okra plant and here it is a few months later and the okra plant has grown to 6 feet tall and is healthy and producing fruit.

The reason I share this story is because there are many lives in this world that have a broken past and they feel like their lives have been uprooted and discarded, just like the okra plant being thrown in the trash, and many of them it seems can't let go of the past and so therefore their future isn't good either but Yeshua through me is telling you not to measure your future by the hurts and problems of your past. Look at the past of the okra plant. I pulled it out of the ground and I treated it like it was a weed and threw it away with all of the other weeds and in the trash can it lay there looking lifeless and hopeless but then someone came along and took the lifeless looking okra plant out of the trash can and replanted it and here it is a few months later and this okra plant that was pulled out of the ground and thrown into the trash is now alive, healthy, 6 feet tall, and producing fruit and so if you are someone with a broken past and it seems like your life has been uprooted and discarded then just allow your life to be replanted in The Fertile Soil of Yeshua The Messiah and allow Him to apply His Tender Loving Care to your life and just like the okra plant, you will grow, become healthy, and live!!!

Jeremiah 31:28 "Just as I watched over them to uproot and tear down, to overthrow, destroy, and bring disaster, so will I also watch over them to build and replant!"

HOW MUCH YESHUA LOVES US

There is not enough measuring cups in the whole wide world
To measure The Amount of Love Yeshua has for you and me
Because if His Love were a liquid
It would be more than the oceans and the seas

If His Love came in the form of rain
Then it would rain every single day
And The Rain of His Love would be much greater than the flood
That washed the whole world away

And we would not need an ark to sail in His Love
Although we would drown in The Love that He gives
For His Love is The Boat that sails us to shore
And His Love is All that we need to live

MY BROTHER'S KEEPER

I will try not to write from experience
Or from the memories of a bad dream
I will try not to tell you about the problems of my life
And how some things have fallen apart at the seams

But I will tell you about my wishes
And about all of the dreams that I want to come true
I will tell you about my heart's desires
But first I must know about you

For you are my brother and my sister
I am my brother's keeper and you are mine
I must know about your heart's desires
And if you cry then I'll wipe a tear from your eye

If you want to talk then I will listen
If you want to listen then I will talk
If you want my opinion then I will give it
And if you ask me to then I will walk

I will walk with you for 1 mile
And if I must then I'll walk 2
I will carry your burdens if you have them
And I will do what I can to help you through

For the question is, "Am I my brother's keeper?"
And the answer is, "Yes, I surely am."
And The Greatest Example was at The Cross
Where they drove the nails through Yeshua's Hands

MORE THAN ME ACCEPTING YESHUA

My name was chosen amongst many
It was not chosen first or chosen last
I don't even know if it was erased and written again
But somehow I was able to pass

I was able to pass through The Gates of Heaven
And to walk down The Streets of Gold
I was able to look in The Face of Yeshua
And All of His Glory I was able to behold

I saw angels and I saw mansions
I saw a smile on everyone's face
I saw a child walking a lion
And then I wondered how I made it to this place

For no good that I ever did
Was good enough to let me in
Except for when I called upon The Name of Yeshua
And I accepted Him as my Saviour and Friend

But more than me accepting Yeshua
It is what He did for you and for I
When He gave His Life for us all
And He stretched His Arms and suffered and died

WHAT LOVE IS NOT

If I tell you that I love you
But yet I spit in your face
And when you make a mistake
I do not show any Grace

If you tell me that you are suffering
And you tell me why
But yet I do nothing to help
And you continue to cry

If you have a heavy burden
That is wearing you down
And I do nothing to help
And you always wear a frown

If I have the resources that can help you
But yet I do not lift a hand
And I leave you all alone
And you do not understand

Because I told you that I loved you
Even though I know your pain
And even though I can help
I still allow you to walk through the storm and the rain

I say that I will pray for you
But yet I have all that you need
But I don't want to be bothered
Because I am living comfortably

I do not want to share your sorrow
Or walk a mile in your shoes
All I want to do
Is say a prayer for you

Because your burden is too heavy
I do not want to help you carry your load
And so I will continue to let you
Carry this burden down the road

But I will still tell you that I love you
And that you mean the world to me
But if I do nothing to help
Then the word, "LOVE" doesn't mean a thing

3-FOLDED CORD

How do you know when you're doing what is right
How do you know when you're wrong
How do you sing a song out of tune
And could it still be a happy song

How do you know when you have met that special someone
Will you feel a special way when you do
And when you do what is the feeling that causes you to know
Will you then start singing in tune

And what will be The Message of the song that you sing
Will The Message be in The Chorus or in the verse
Or will The Message be in Both as They stand side by side
And will This be A Song that you'll rehearse

Or will you already know how the Whole Song is played
And will you sing the verse before The Chorus of The Song
And then after you sing The Chorus should you sing another verse
And if you didn't, would It be wrong

For The Message is already spoken in The Chorus and first verse
And so with another verse it may help you to understand
The Message that was given with The Chorus and first verse
For The Chorus and the verses go hand in hand

And so The Message that I believe that I'm trying to speak to you
Is that there's not really a way that you can sing out of tune
For if you sing with a joyful noise Both The Chorus and the verse
Then The Message will become clear very soon,

"That the first and second verse are symbolic to a man and woman
Who shall be joined together and create a wonderful song
And The Chorus is Symbolic to Yeshua our Saviour
Because without Him, it all would be wrong!"

THE QUEST OF LIFE

A search is like a journey
It is like a quest throughout your life
To find an answer to a problem
Or to find a husband or a wife

But in order to find what you are searching for
You must believe and do what is right
You must go by faith and trust in Father Yahweh
And He will direct you to The Light

But please, don't worry about the circumstance
Or what may get in your way
For if you believe and go by faith
Then you will make it to another day

And you will see that going by faith
That you will find the key to open the door
And when you open the door you will find the answer
To the problem that you are searching for

Or maybe you will find something else
Like maybe a husband or a wife
And you will find it in this search or journey
Which is called, "THE QUEST OF LIFE!"

WHEN YOU HAVE FOUND LOVE

I never thought that the day would come
When all of my dreams came true
When I would reach for the stars and grab a hold
And be able to make it through

But I have learned in my life to accomplish your dreams
Or to reach for the brightest star
You must first find Love and then you will see
Just who you really are

For Love is The Root of All Good Things
Love is like a Tiny Seed
That needs to be watered and nourished everyday
So that you can have all that you need

For without Love your dreams will never come true
You'll never be able to reach for the brightest star
And without Love you will never know
Just who you really are

But when you do find out who you are
And all of your dreams start to come true
When you reach for the stars and you grab a hold
Then you know that you will make it through

And when you find that special someone whom you care for
And you know that you can love them from deep within
Then congratulations my friend for you have just found Love
And that is The Beginning Without An End

YOU CANNOT BUT FIND LOVE

"It cannot but happen!"
I heard the old man say
But when I asked him what he was talking about
He just turned and walked away

He never answered my question
He just left without a word
Then all of a sudden, down from the sky
Came a Beautiful White Bird

And the bird, it flew stationary
Maybe 10 feet in front of my eyes
Then all of a sudden it flew away
And disappeared into the night sky

And then I stood there in amazement
And I wondered at what it meant
And then I started to understand
The message the old man sent

And I realized that the old man
He wasn't a man after all
But he was An Angel sent from Heaven
And then I understood the White Bird that I saw

And The White Bird, It was just Confirmation
For It was The Holy Spirit from Above
And The Message was, "If you keep the faith
Then you cannot but find love!!!"

TRUE LOVE

There once was a man
Who did not have much in his life
Until one day he met this girl
And she later became his wife

She was more than he had ever dreamed of
She was worth more than money could buy
And her love to him was like the sun
Shining bright up in the sky

She was like a guardian angel
That was sent from Heaven Above
Because of the life that she gave to him
And because of her love

But he often wondered what would happen
And he often wondered what she would do
If he ever left this world before her
If she would be able to make it through

But one day he did die
And his wife's heart was broken into
All she had left was the memories
To help her make it through

But she always remembered the love
That he always gave to her
It was like a fish in the ocean
And like a wing on a bird

But he always made sure while he was alive
That he never did her wrong
And he gave her enough love to last her
Because he knew one day he would be gone

CROSSING THE BORDER/DESTINY

There once was a man who was walking along a trail
And as he was walking he found several pennies in a pale
He turned the pennies into quarters
And then he traveled to the border
And he married a Mexican wife

He met her on that same day
As he was crossing the border she was coming his way
She was carrying a heavy sack
And so he put it on his back
And he walked with her to her home

As they were walking she had a smile on her face
Because she was so happy that he was coming to her place
When they walked into her house
Everyone was as quiet as a mouse
And they were all very happy when they saw the young man

The young lady had 3 sisters and a brother
And then walked in her father and her mother
There was so much excitement in her voice
That her parents knew she had found Father Yahweh's Choice
And they knew that it wasn't just love at first sight

For she had met him on that same day
As he was crossing the border she was coming his way
She was carrying a heavy sack
And so he put it on his back
And he walked with her to her home

When her parents walked in they saw the young man
Her father smiled at him and he shook his hand
Her mother gave him a hug
And then she sat on a rug
And when she sat down she had tears in her eyes

Her father spoke Spanish to the young man
But the young man, he could not understand
Nor did he know why
The mother had tears in her eyes
Nor why the father had a smile on his face

And then the father took his daughter's and the young man's hand
And then the young man, he began to understand
Why the father still had a smile on his face
And why he was still at their place
And why the mother had tears of joy within her eyes

For the father and mother had prayed earlier that day
That Father Yahweh would send a young man their daughter's way
A young man who would help their daughter out
And then they would know without a doubt
That this young man was created just for her

And then the daughter smiled at her father and mother
And she also smiled at her sisters and brother
And then she took the young man's hand
And then he finally started to understand
That his destiny was beginning to unfold

For they had met one another on that same day
As he was crossing the border she was walking his way
She was carrying a heavy sack
And so he placed it upon his back
And then they walked together to their home

CHAOTIC WORLD/DESTINY

Somewhere in this chaotic world
Two people were lost at sea
Both with a destination in mind
But a little uncertain that they would find

For the wind started to blow
And the rain started to fall
And it took a while for them
To realize their call

For they hadn't yet realized
That when the wind and the rain came
That Father Yahweh was at work
And He knew them both by name

One was sailing from the east
The other one was sailing from the west
And they both were doing their best
To get to a place where they could rest

For they remembered that the Next Day, It was The Sabbath
And so now they understood the meaning of it all
They understood the wind and the rain
And they understood their call

And they realized that the meaning of their search
Was leading them to what was meant to be
And they realized that there was a reason
They both were lost at sea

For one of them was shipwrecked
And the other one was battling the wind
And the one who was battling the wind
Was sent to rescue a friend

For the one who was still in his boat
Rescued the lady who was shipwrecked at sea
And then immediately afterwards the wind and the rain quit
And then they realized that it was meant to be

And then the sun came out
And a gentle breeze blew
And then they looked at each other
For in their hearts they knew

And then they looked on ahead
And they were surprised when they saw land
And then they knew in their hearts
That this was all part of The Master's Plan

For as The Sabbath drew near
Together they sailed into shore
And when they arrived
They received so much more

They received more than they had imagined
For they knew that they were going to be husband and wife
And they knew that where they were was the place
Where they would spend the rest of their life

For they were greeted by many friendly faces
And for The Sabbath they had a place to rest
And then they thanked Father Yahweh for everything that had happened
For it all had turned out to be for the very best

THE SEVENTH DAY

The 7th Day is Father Yahweh's Special Day
That we read about in His Book
It is The Only Day that He set aside and called, "Holy!"
And if you don't believe me then just take a look

It is 1 of 10 Commandments
And It is The 4th from The Top of The List
It is The Only One that says, "Remember,,,"
And It is The One that most Christians miss

For most of us have gotten caught up on earning money
And getting all of our projects done
That we never rest on The Same Day
As The Father and Son

But there's A Reason The Commandment says, "Remember,,,"
Because Father Yahweh knew that It would be forgotten one day
It would be forgotten by those who say they love Him
And they just treat everyday the same

But if you look in James ch. 2 It says
That if you say you keep The Whole Law
But yet you stumble in One Point
You are still guilty of All

It says in Hebrews ch. 4
That Father Yahweh designates A Certain Day
And It speaks of The 7th Day
In Exactly This Way,

"That Father Yahweh rested The 7th Day
From all the works He had done
He Blessed The Sabbath and called It, 'Holy!'
So let us do The Same as The Father and Son

Let us therefore be diligent to enter That Rest
Lest anyone amongst us should fall
Let us keep The Commandments of Father Yahweh
And let us, "Remember," to keep Them All

THE TRUTH SHALL SET YOU FREE

The Garden of Eden
Was the first home on earth
And the 2 people who lived there
Never came from natural birth

They were created in The Image of our Heavenly Father
Father Yahweh breathed into Adam the breath of life
And then from Adam Father Yahweh took a rib
And He made Adam a wife

They were created to have fellowship with Father Yahweh
And to take care of the ground
And they did really well
Until a serpent came snooping around

And then Eve was deceived by the serpent
And she ate from the fruit of the tree
And then she offered it to Adam
And then they were no longer free

For Father Yahweh had told them not to eat from the tree
Or death would surely come
And so when Adam and Eve heard The Voice of Father Yahweh
They were afraid and started to run

For they knew that they were naked
And that their freedom was taken away
And that their fellowship with Father Yahweh was ruined
Once satan had come their way

For Eve listened to the lie that satan told her
And Adam listened to his wife
And then their fellowship with Father Yahweh was ruined
And a curse came upon all life

So don't you listen to the lies that satan tells you
Just listen to Father Yahweh and you will see
That your life with Him will always be full
Because The Truth shall set you free

STAND

Whoever builds their house without Yeshua
Is like one who builds upon the sand
And then when the wind and the rain blow in
The house is not able to stand

For the foundation is very weak
And it easily moves and shakes
And so whatever is built upon this foundation
It is built upon a mistake

But whoever builds their house with Yeshua
Then on The Solid Rock it shall stand
And it will be unmovable
For its Foundation is not sand

Its Foundation is Firm and Strong
And It doesn't move and shake
And so whatever is built upon This Foundation
It is not built upon a mistake

And so my friend, be Steadfast and Firm
And Stay Fully Devoted to doing what is right
Always labor and labor not in vain
And be strong with all of your might

For your Strength and your Foundation is Yeshua
And so listen to His Command
Be Steadfast, Firm, and Strong
And above all, "STAND!"

RADICAL WORSHIP

I will jump up and down and I will lift my hands
And I will raise my voices so high
That not even gravity can hold it down
And it will reach past the sky

It will burst through the stars and the galaxies
And it will go far beyond the milky way
It will travel faster than the speed of light
For it will be A Voice of Praise

I will sing a song and I will Praise His Name
And I will declare His Wonderful Works and deeds
And I will tell others about Who Yeshua is
And I will plant many seeds

For the harvest is plentiful but the laborers are few
And so I must be Radical in all that I do
For others are watching and I want them to know
This Joy that I'm experiencing too

So whether I sing or whether I dance
Or I raise my hands and clap them high
I want others to know that I'm sending my Praise
Far beyond the sky

And if my Praises could be seen on a radar screen
Then surely the screen would explode
For it would not have the strength to contain all of the excitement
And it would cause an overload

And so my friends, let us be Radical in our Worship and Praise
So that everyone around us can see
They can see how happy we truly are
And they will see Yeshua in you and in me

THE BREAD OF LIFE

When I looked up in the sky I didn't see a bird
I didn't see any birds on the ground
And so I just walked in the store and I bought a loaf of bread
And then when I threw the bread many birds came flying down

They gathered all around and they ate up all of the bread
And I was very surprised by what I did see
Because before when I looked up there wasn't even one bird in sight
But then when I threw the bread there were plenty

For when I threw the first piece of bread not even a second later
The first bird came flying down
And then came another and another and another
Until many birds were eating from off the ground

And then I wondered about what had just happened
And was there a message that Father Yahweh wanted me to see
Because before when I looked up there wasn't even one bird in sight
But then when I threw the bread there were plenty

There were plenty of birds, all different kinds
That were eating the food from off the ground
And then as I was watching I saw many more
Many more birds gathering around

And then I thought about the message that was being taught
Right before my very eyes
And the message came from me throwing the bread
And many birds coming down from the sky

And so in this life The Bread is The Word
The Bread is The Father and The Son
And if you give This Bread to all who are hungry
Then the harvest will surely come

THE DEVINE MAKEOVER

Our history does not determine our future
Whatever happened before, it is in the past
And so we must go forward and trust in Yeshua
And allow Yeshua to be First and we be Last

We must always think of others more than ourselves
Because this is what we are commanded to do
We must always love and never be selfish
And we must do what we can to help others through

Because we are moving forward in Yeshua's Name
Whatever happened before, it is in the past
That is why we are going forward and trusting in Yeshua
And allowing Yeshua to be first while we are last

We must always think of others more than ourselves
We should never do anything out of selfishness or pride
Because the difference between then and now is Who's I am
And now I am on The Right Side

Because The Devine Demolition has been completed
The Devine Makeover was destined to be
Yeshua cleaned me up when I asked for forgiveness
And He cast all of my sins into the sea

The sea that is called, "Forgetfulness."
No one fishes there day or night
Because there are no fish in that sea that are swimming around
And there are no birds over that sea that are in flight

And I am so glad that our history doesn't determine our future
And whatever happened before, it stays in the past
And so we must always go forward and trust in Yeshua
And allow Yeshua to be first and we be last

REACHING YOUR DESTINATION

It's not only the destination
But it's the journey along the way
For it's the journey that builds your character
And makes you stronger everyday

It helps to increase your knowledge
In everything you say and do
You will learn what it means to become stronger
And that you will make it through

There will be rocks along the pathway
Some will be big and some will be small
But if you look at it as, "It's part of the journey."
Then you will learn to stand strong and tall

For it doesn't matter how huge the rock is
Or how long the valley may be
If you always look at it as, "It's part of the journey."
Then you will always be happy

And then when you reach your destination
And you think back to yesterday
And you look at all that you went through
And how it made you stronger everyday

And it helped to sharpen your character
And it taught you what to say and do
It taught you to be strong in Yeshua
And how to make it through

POT OF GOLD

The other day I was so happy when I walked outside
And the sun, it was shining so bright
Then all of a sudden tears fell from my eyes
As I stood beneath the sunlight

And when the light of the sun hit my tears
What a beautiful sight that I saw
For I saw the colors of a rainbow right before my eyes
And I wasn't scared at all

For I was reminded of The Promise that Father Yahweh had made
I was reminded to be still
And be patient on Father Yahweh and be anxious for nothing
And to always do His Perfect Will

For good things will come if I am faithful
But I must do more than just believe
For even the demons believe but yet they tremble
And they have many tricks up their sleeve

And so I must believe with all of my might
And I must learn what it takes to be strong
I must go by faith and not by sight
And then nothing will ever go wrong

For I will learn what it takes to walk through the valley
And to walk up the steepest hill
I will learn what it takes to climb the mountain
And to do Father Yahweh's Perfect Will

And then when I get to the end of the road
And just before my life is through
My Heavenly Father will look at me and say,
"My son, I am so very proud of you!

For you accomplished a trial of faith
And you learned what it takes to be strong
And even though you walked through several valleys
You learned that nothing was wrong.

For it was in those times that you learned the most.
You learned how to hold onto Me tight.
You learned what it takes to win the race
And to go by faith and not by sight.

And so the next time that you cry tears of joy
What A Beautiful Sight that you'll behold
For you will see more than just the colors of a rainbow
But you will see your POT OF GOLD!"

A DIAMOND IN THE ROUGH

Rejoice when you go through the fire
Rejoice when your faith is being tried
Rejoice when persecution comes
Because that is when you are being pressurized

Just like a diamond when it is being formed
It must be pressurized through the fire and heat
And so if we can Rejoice when we are being tried
Then just like the diamond, we'll become beautiful and neat

For it is in the trials that we go through
And the persecutions that we face
That help determine just what we're made of
And if we are treating others with Mercy and Grace

And so just as Yeshua is looking down at us
With Compassion and Mercy in His Eyes
And with His Grace He has forgiven us
And so what we do unto others should be no big surprise

We should Forgive those who persecute us
We should show Grace and Mercy everyday
For it is in these times that our faith is being tried
And we are being formed like a diamond everyday

And so Rejoice when you are being persecuted
Stand Solid for Yeshua all of the time
Always praise Yeshua even when your skies seem dark
For this is when your faith is being tried

And so just like a diamond, you are being pressurized
You must go through the fire and the heat
And if you keep your faith in Yeshsua and always believe
Then you'll be pressurized like a diamond and become beautiful and neat

A GAME OF POKER

Life is like a game of poker
You must play the cards in which you are dealt
You must choose wisely with the cards that you keep
And discard the ones that will melt

That will melt you away from The Solid Foundation
Just like ice melts when it doesn't stay cold
And you must always choose to do what is right
Because if you don't then you'd be better off to fold

To fold the hand that was dealt to you
No matter how good or bad it may seem to be
For if you discard and keep wisely
Then eventually you will see

You will see that with faith and making the right decisions
The bad will be turned into good
And you will see that making the right decisions
Will cause your life to be lived the way that it should

For the cards in your life are the events that happen
And so you must make the right decision in everything you do
You must choose to keep the good and do away with the bad
And the only one who can do this is you

For your life is like a game of poker
You must do away with the bad and always keep the good
You must choose wisely in every decision you make
And then your life will be lived the way that it should

A SMALL SHEPHERD BOY

King David was a small shepherd boy
He was the youngest of Jessie's sons
He was the one who defeated Goliath
And then all of the Philistines started to run

For they knew that their champion was dead
And they knew they were defeated that day
They thought they could never be beat
But Father Yahweh used a small shepherd boy to make them run away

For the Philistines had insulted the armies of Father Yahweh
And their champion was very tall in height
But Father Yahweh used a small shepherd boy
To show the world His Power and Might

For the small shepherd boy did not wear any armor
Nor did he have any mighty weapons in his hand
All he had was a slingshot and 5 smooth stones
But it only took one stone to knock down the very tall and strong man

And so my friend, you may not be a very strong person
Nor very tall in height
But remember, Father Yahweh can use the weak and the small
To show the world His Power and Might

For King David, he was a small shepherd boy
He was much too small to fight a mighty tall and strong man
But Father Yahweh used him to knock down a giant
With just a slingshot and a stone in his hand

FIGHT THE GOOD FIGHT

When you feel like you are on a roller coaster
Because your life goes up and down
When you feel like your life is just existence
And you always wear a frown

When it seems as though you don't have a purpose
And the meaning of life has vanished away
Just remember that there is always struggles
Sometimes everyday

But never give up, never give in
Never quit the fight
Put together the broken pieces of the puzzle
So each piece fits exactly right

Also put in the struggles to the puzzle
For that piece must always go in
For if you never learn from your struggles then you'll never learn what it takes
To make it to the end

For it is better to start in the bottom of the valley
Than it is to start up in the sky
For if you start in the valley then you will learn what it takes
To make it upon high

But if you start in the sky and you drop down to the valley
Then you're not going to know what to do
For you never experienced or learned what it takes
To make it up through the white and the blue

So my friend, never give up, never give in
Always fight the good fight
Run the race and run it well
Go by faith and not by sight

BUILDING YOUR FOUNDATION UPON FAITH

When things sometimes happen
And it seems kind of strange
When things fall together
And everything starts to change

When you think that it's a coincidence
Because you don't think it could happen to you
Well let me tell you from experience
If you believe, it will come true

It may take a while
For everything to fall into place
But I can guarantee you that you'll be a winner
If you build your foundation upon faith

You will come out on top
And you will make it through it all
Just as long as you believe
And you're not afraid to fall

Just believe in Yeshua
And He will see you through
And then when you make it to the top of the mountain
All of your dreams will come true

BORROWED TIME

Many times I have often wondered
Is this time that I'm living, is it mine
Is this time going to last forever
Or is this time borrowed time

Because if it's my time then I will live forever
But if it's borrowed time then I don't have long
So I better hurry up and do what I have to do
So when I leave this world I'll be sure to go Home

And There, my time, it won't be borrowed
But There, the time, it will be mine
Because There, I will live forever
I won't be living on borrowed time

I will be living on The Time that Yeshua purchased
Because Salvation, It is Free
So if you are not saved then you better hurry up
Because borrowed time don't last for eternity

AND THEN WHAT

A little boy and a preacher
Was walking down the road one day
And the preacher, well
He had many things to say

He said, "Son,
What are you going to do when you get older?"
And the little boy said,
"I want to join the army and be a soldier."

And then the preacher asked,
"What will you do when your service is through?"
And the little boy said,
"There is a lot of things that I would like to do."

"What's one of the things?" the preacher asked.
He was really wanting to know
And the little boy said,
"I'd like to make lots of money and be in a lot of t.v. shows."

"I want to be rich and famous
And have my name spread throughout the land
I want to have a home and a car
And I want to be my own man."

And then the preacher asked,
"What will you do when all of this is through?"
And the little boy said,
"I guess I'll settle down and get married and maybe have a kid or two."

And then the preacher asked,
"What will your next move be?"
And the little boy said,
"Well, me and my family, we'll travel the country."

"I'll watch my kids as they grow up
And I'll take them to a lot of my shows."
"And then what?" the preached asked.
And the little boy said, "Well, I don't know."

"I guess I'll take my family on home
And put my kids through school
And I'll even teach my kids
The golden rule."

"And then one day my kids, they'll get married
And I'll watch them as they start a family
And then maybe they'll have some kids
And they'll call me granddaddy."

"And I'll watch my grandkids as they play
And they'll probably fall a few times and get a few cuts.
And me, well I'll just grow old and die."
And the preacher said, "And then what?"

SUBTITLE: THE STAMP

A little boy was walking home from school one day
With a letter in his hand
And on his way home he stopped at the post office
And there he talked to the mailman

The little boy said, "Sir, how are you today?
I have a letter that I would like to send."
"Well who are you sending it to?" the mailman asked.
And the little boy said, "To a dear, dear friend."

"Well that's a mighty big letter," the mailman replied.
"How far does it have to go?"
"It's got to go a far way," the little boy said.
"And it will cost some money I know."

"Well who is your friend and where does he live?"
The mailman asked, even though he knew
And the little boy pointed his finger way up in the sky and said,
"He lives beyond the white and the blue."

"Well who is your friend?" the mailman asked again.
And the little boy answered with such delight!
"My Friend, His Name is Yeshua
And in The Bible He gave the blind man his sight."

"And in this letter I just want to thank Yeshua
For giving me a home and a mommy and a pappy
And Mr. Mailman, well I just want to let Him know
That I couldn't be more happy!"

"So Mr. Mailman, how much will it be?
I don't have much money but you can have this notebook wire."
And the mailman just patted the little boy on the head and said,
"Son, NO POSTAGE REQUIRED!"

THE DEBT

A debt was started a long time ago
A debt that man could not pay
It was a debt that got started because of sin
And the debt became larger everyday

It could not be paid by money or good works
But it could only be paid by The Blood of The Lamb
And The Lamb is The Shepherd, The Creator of all
And He came in the form of man

He humbled Himself for you and for I
He came not only as our Master but as our Friend
He lived A Perfect and Spotless Life and He came to teach us
How we could be saved from the penalty of sin

But in order to save us This Perfect and Spotless Lamb
Had to shed His Blood as He hung upon a tree
But it didn't stop there because there was just one more thing
That had to be done for you and for me

For after the shedding of His Blood was completed
And the penalty for sin was paid
Three days later He unlocked the chains of death
When He arose and walked out of the grave

And so now the rest is up to you and me
Will we accept Yeshua as our Saviour and Friend
Will we live our life completely for Yeshua
And let His Love be The Message we send

For He showed us His Love when He gave up His Life
And He paid a debt that He didn't owe
He shed His Blood when He suffered and died
And then 3 days later He Arose!

THE HIGHEST COURT

There is Another Court
That lies outside of this world
And It is The Court that will decide
Our ultimate and final reward

And in This Court satan will be against
Every man and woman's soul
He will be against all of those who love Yeshua
And everyone's death is his ultimate goal

He stands in The Courts of Heaven
With Yeshua on The Other Side
Telling The Judge why we all deserve death
Because we all stole, murdered, and lied

But then The Righteous Lawyer will step forward and say
Whatever sins they may have done
They were forgiven and forgotten when they asked and believed
By the shedding of My Blood

And so a pardon will be granted
And life eternal we will receive
Life with Yeshua for all eternity
Will be The Reward we will achieve

And then sin and evil will be destroyed
And the wicked will be no more
And then all of us who live for Yeshua
Will walk through Heaven's Doors

THE RACE

To everybody there is someone
To every dream there is an open door
To every mountain there is a ladder of faith
And to every sea there is a shore

To every road there is a traveler
To every home there is a heart
To every heart broken there is a tear
And before you finish you must start

You must start to learn how to find that someone
You must learn how to walk through that open door
You must go by faith and climb the mountain
And you must sail your boat into the shore

For you are the traveler who is on that road
And Home, (Heaven,) is where you hang your heart
And at Home, (Heaven,) no hearts are broken
And the tears from your eyes will never start

Because to every race there is a beginning
And to every beginning there must be an end
But to finish The Race you must hold Hands
With Yeshua, our Truest Friend

For I did not come to start The Race
For The Race was started long ago
But I came to finish The Race with my Saviour
And at the end it will show

That I, I was a traveler
And I started with a broken heart
But I went by faith through the right doors
That was predestined from the start

And on the way I will find that someone
Because I will keep going by faith through the right doors
And because I am going by faith then I will keep climbing the mountain
And I will keep sailing my boat into the shore

And so you see, The Race was already started
It was started long ago
And so I did not come to start but to finish The Race
And at the end it will surely show

For The Grace of Father Yahweh is in my life
Because I invited Yeshua into my heart
And when the doors of my heart came open wide
That is when my race began to start

But like I said, "The Race had already started.
It had started long ago.
And so I did not come to start but to finish The Race
Because The Grace of Father Yahweh has made me whole!"

THE ROAD TO DAMASCUS

Has your heart ever had evil intentions
Have you always wanted to do what you knew was right
And as you were on that journey to fulfill what was in your heart
Did something cause you to stop and see the light

Well that is what happened to the apostle Paul
He was going to persecute The Christians that day
His heart was full of evil intentions
But something stopped him along the way

As he journeyed A Bright Light that shown from Heaven
Caused him to fall to the ground
And the men who journeyed with Paul were speechless
Because all that they heard was a sound

When Paul stood up he couldn't see a thing
And so he was led into Damascus that day
For 3 days he was made to be blind
And so Yeshua sent someone his way

Ananias said, "Paul, in The Name of Yeshua
Receive The Holy Spirit and receive your sight!"
And all of this happened soon after Paul journeyed to Damascus
And he fell to the ground after seeing That Bright Light

And so my friend, have you ever been on that road to Damascus
Did you ever have evil intentions within your heart
And did something happen that caused you to fall to the ground
And the evil intentions in your heart started to depart

And you realized that it was on that road to Damascus
It was on that road where you and I saw That Bright Light
And we saw That Bright Light because we were blind
But soon afterwards we received our sight!!!

HOLDING ONTO THE FUTURE

Everything is falling together
Everything is falling in place
Soon the future will be here
And the past will be erased

For what the future holds is something good
Just as long as I believe
And what the past has taken is just a few years of my life
And so today is all that I need

For the past is already gone
But the future is yet to come
But my future is what I make it
Which way will I run

Will I run in the way that I've already lived
Or will I run in the way that I should
Will I dream a dream and run towards the future
And hold on to something that is good

For if I hold onto the past then it will drag me down
But if I hold onto the future then the day will come
When all of my dreams come true and I know in my heart
That I will nevermore have to run

But I will still hold onto the future
For the future is just a second away
And I will let go of the past and then I will be glad
That I ran the other way

THE UNSEEN KEY

I was searching for an answer
I was searching for a key
I was searching for a door
That would cause me to be free

But I had to find the key that would open the door
And that seemed like the hardest thing to do
But when I found the key the door came open
And so I thought I would walk on through

I walked through the door without the answer
Even though I thought that the answer was the key
But the key only opened the door
The key never caused me to be free

And so I searched and searched and searched
But the answer I could not find
But then all of a sudden
A thought ran through my mind

And the thought was, "Don't just dream and don't just search,,,"
",,,but let your dream come to life and live!"
For if you live your dream then your search is over
And then to yourself you will give

You will give to yourself the answer
And the insight to what life is about
You will live your dream and not just wish it
And you will hear a silent shout

And then you will find The Key that you cannot see
And you will walk through The Door you never knew
But you won't need the answer for The Answer, (Yeshua,) is The Key, (Yeshua)
That caused you to walk on through

For before the key wasn't the answer
And the answer wasn't the key
For the key you had was only physical
It could never allow you to be free

For that key only fit one door
And that door was one that you saw
And you could walk through that door without The Answer, (Yeshua)
And you could easily stumble and fall

But then when you found The Answer, (Yeshua,) that caused you to find
The Key, (Yeshua,) that you could not see
Then you opened The Door that you never knew
And That Key, (Yeshua,) caused you to be free

Because before That Door came open
Your silent shouts were heard with many sounds
But then when you opened The Door with The Unseen Key, (Yeshua)
There was a moment of silence all around

ASK, SEEK, KNOCK

If you knock the door will open
If you seek you will surely find
If you ask you'll receive the answers
That you've been searching for with your heart and mind

If you climb you will climb the mountain
And you may carry a heavy load
If you travel you will travel the highway
That leads you to that open road

If you walk you will find the pathway
That leads you to that open door
And when you walk through after climbing the mountain
Then in your heart you will have definitely scored

You will have scored victory in the height of that mountain
And you will have found The Answer on that open road
You will have met Yeshua out on that pathway
The One Who always helped you carry your load

And then you will be thankful for all that you went through
For it helped to make you strong
And then you will see that when it was hard
It was never, ever wrong

PROVE ME NOW

Prove Me now herewith saith Father Yahweh
And see what I will do
For if you pay all of your tithes
Then this I promise you

I will open up The Windows of Heaven
So much that you will not be able to receive
All of the blessings that will be poured out to you
And all of this by your faith you will have achieved

Prove me now herewith saith Father Yahweh
I believe means more than just paying your tithes
But it can also mean for when we pray
And we talk to Father Yahweh with open or closed eyes

A TIME IN MY LIFE

There was a time in my life when I was homeless
Even though I had a roof over my head
And there was a time in my life when I had no place to sleep
Even though I laid upon a bed

There was a time in my life when I did not have a dream
Even though I dreamed every night
And there was a time in my life when I could not see a thing
But nothing was wrong with my sight

And there was a time in my life when the road I was traveling
Seemed all uphill
And there was a time in my life when I didn't know what it meant
To do Father Yahweh's Perfect Will

For the time in my life when I was homeless
Even though I had a roof over my head
It was at a time in my life when I had no faith
And so inside I was spiritually dead

And the time in my life when I did not have a dream
Even though I dreamed every night
It was at a time in my life when I had no vision
And I did not know of any hope in sight

And the time in my life when I had no place to sleep
Even though I laid upon a bed
It was at a time in my life when I was tossing and turning
While several thoughts were going through my head

And the time in my life when I could not see a thing
Even though nothing was wrong with my sight
It was at a time in my life when I was walking in darkness
And so I could not see the light

And so the time in my life when I was homeless
And I had no place to sleep
That was when I learned to pray and say, "Father Yahweh,,,"
",,, take my soul to keep."

And the time in my life when I did not have a dream
And I could not see a thing
That was when I learned to lift my voice
And sing Praises to The King

And so when I found myself walking along the way
Searching for the open door
That was at a time in my life when I was dead
But now I am alive forever more

I REMEMBER THE TIME

Is this something that I have created
Are these dreams that my memory holds
Or did these events really happen
And has my life started to unfold

Am I living the life that Father Yahweh has predestined
Am I doing what is right day by day
Well these are just a few questions that go through my mind
As I think of yesterday

For I remember a time when I knew there had to be more
To life than what I saw
I remember there had to be more to Yeshua than what people were
showing me
And so I decided to follow my call

I remember a time when I learned what it meant
To deny myself everyday
And I remember a time what it felt like to reach for the stars
And to go by faith every step of the way

I remember a time what it felt like
To walk through an open door
I remember a time what it felt like
To sail my boat into the shore

And I remember a time when I received a blessing
And I said, "Yeshua, Thank You."
And I remember a time when I heard Yeshua say,
"No, thank you."

MY LIFE LIVED/MY HOPE FOR TOMORROW

I will tell you a story
About the life I have lived
About the things I have offered
And the things I have gived

I will tell you all about
The life that I have gained
Of the things I have accomplished
And how it's not been in vain

I will tell you what it took
For all of my dreams to come true
I will tell you how I lived
And how I made it through

I will tell you how I gave
And I will tell you how I received
And then I will tell you of everything
That I know that I'll achieve

For the outcome of this moment
Is because of the last
And the outcome of my future
Will be the result of my past

For my life goes where ever I take it
And my dreams will go as high as the sky
My reach will extend beyond tomorrow
And you may see a Tear of Joy within my eye

And then you may ask me why I am so happy
For you may see no reason why I am happy at all
And then I will tell you that I know my Future, (IN HEAVEN)
And how to get back up after a fall

I will tell you my Hope for tomorrow, (Yeshua!)
And I will tell you my dream for today
And then I will tell you why I am so happy
As I travel along life's way

For what I have received, it is just an outcome
Of the things that I did give
And what I gave was just The Message
The Message of Yeshua's Life Lived!

PAST, PRESENT, FUTURE

Soon the future will be the present
Soon the present will be the past
But the past will never be lived
But the memories will always last

For we will all live the present and future
But the past will soon swallow it all
For the present only last a second
And the future, well, it's your call

Because your future is what you make it
So live today as best as you can
For what you do today will be the result for tomorrow
And this is true for every man

For the future will soon be in the present
And the present will soon be in the past
And the past is what makes your history
And then the future just comes too fast

A WONDERFUL WORLD

What a wonderful world
This would be
If everyone saw you for you
And they saw me for me

If they didn't look at the appearance
That may be upon our face
But they saw each of us as an Image
Of Father Yahweh's Wonderful Grace

If they didn't look at the outside
Or at the way that we may walk
But they looked on the inside
And they heard the way we talked

If everyone were blind
And they could not see
Then they would truly see you for you
And they would see me for me

WHO IS MY NEIGHBOR

I will tell you from the beginning
What this poem is about
That way when you get to the end
There should not be a doubt

Every person that crosses our path
Is our neighbor and our friend
They are our friends for life
And our neighbors until the end

They are there for us to help
In the biggest and the smallest ways
We should love them as we love ourselves
And be willing to help them everyday

Because The Greatest Commandment is to Love Father Yahweh
With all of our heart, with all of our soul, and with all of mind
And then to love thy neighbor as thyself
It is The Greatest Love we will ever find

"And who is my neighbor?" you may ask
Well they are the people that we see
They are the people walking by
And passing you and me

So now that I have told you from the beginning
What this poem is about
Now that we are at the end
There should not be a doubt

Every person that crosses our path
Is our neighbor and our friend
They are our friends for life
And our neighbors until the end

WHAT IS HUNGER

Hunger is an emptiness
It can be either bad or good
It can help you to make the right decisions
So your life will be lived the way that it should

Do not be hungry for the things of this earth
For all those things will pass away
But always be hungry for Holiness
And The Joy that It brings will never fade away

Be Holy in all manner of conversation
Bridle your tongue and always speak what is good
Always tell others about Yeshua
And speak the things that you should

But don't only teach by word
But teach by action and deed
Be Holy as Yeshua is Holy
And may Yeshua use you to plant many seeds

Let your hunger always be for Holiness
Let it come from deep within your soul
Share with others as you have received
And It will make your life whole!!!

IN ORDER TO KNOW YESHUA

All of my life has set me up
For what I am doing today
For in my life I have been through some challenges
But I knew there was a better way

For all of my life I heard about Yeshua
Just trust in Him and you'll make it through
But I never really saw anything of what I heard
And so in a way I knew just what to do

That's when I started searching
And then I started to find
That's when I started knocking
And the doors came open wide

And what I found was the direction
That Father Yahweh would use in my life
And when I walked through the doors I received the blessings
And I learned how to become strong through the trouble and strife

When I asked I received answers
Because I went by faith each step of the way
And when I seeked I met myself
Along my own pathway

And when I found out who I was
The life that Father Yahweh predestined for me
That was when I learned more about Yeshua
And now I am starting to see

That in order to know Who Yeshua is
You must first find out who you are
You must follow the blueprints that Father Yahweh has for you
And then you will learn how to reach for the stars

And what I mean is you'll learn to go by faith
You'll learn to trust in Father Yahweh every single day
And then when you find yourself, then you'll already know Yeshua
Because you have trusted in Him to lead your way

So in order to know Yeshua you must first know yourself
The life that Father Yahweh has predestined for you
And the reason I know is because I know who I am
And I hope that you do too

IT IS WRITTEN

Many people continue to talk
About what they think is right
When all you have to do is read The Bible
And there you will see The Light

They will argue with you when you tell them The Truth
And they will say that you are strange
But don't dislike them because they are different
Because we all have room to change

I know because I used to be part
Of this world that we live in today
I was lost and undone and I never would listen
To anything that the Christians had to say

I would argue with them and tell them they were wrong
And I always thought that I was right
I never really learned anything about The Gospel
Until one cold, dark night

And I found myself not knowing where to go
I found myself lost in sin
And then I found myself reading The Bible
And I found my Truest Friend

And I found that The Answers that I thought were wrong
Are Surely True and Right
And now I live each day witnessing to people
And I try to help them see The Light

And many times they will argue with me
Especially when they are sittin'
But I just tell them, Don't argue with me
For in The Bible IT IS WRITTEN!"

LIKE A DRUMMER IN A BAND

The reason that we take test
Is to determine how much we know
If we know a lot then our grade will be high
And if not, then it will be low

But in life as we take a test
We usually learn as we are taking it and not before
And we don't get graded by our teachers at school
And then when the bell rings we run out the door

Because usually as we are taking this test
We are not even aware of what is at hand
Because all we are mindful of is what we are doing
Just like a drummer marching in a band

Because all they are doing is beating their drums
As they are marching in front of a crowd
And they are playing their drums with the sounds of other instruments
And the music must be played very loud

It must be played loud enough so that everyone can hear
But before the music was played to the public the band practiced everyday
And the practice to them was just like taking a test
And they became much better everytime they played

And so remember in life as we are taking test
We usually learn as we are taking them and not before
Because our test in life is mainly living day by day
And trusting in Yeshua to lead us through the right doors

But we must be very careful how we live our lives
Because a test to us may be a message to someone else you see
And the message you send could travel the world
And it could spread for all eternity

SETTING A GOOD EXAMPLE

As I was walking through the field
There I saw a dog
It was feeding its young
Beside an old log

Then I saw a chicken
Laying in a barn
It was laying over its young
Trying to keep them from harm

Then as I climb over a fence
There I saw a bear
It was feeding its young
And keeping them warm with its hair

Then as I walk to the house
There I saw a kid
He was all hurt and heart broken
From what his parents did

And then I started wondering
About the dog, chicken, and bear
Why can't we be more like that
And why can't we care

Why can't we love our children
And keep them from harm
And if they need someone to lean on
Let them lean on your arm

Let's show our children that we love them
And show them that we care
And that we're going to set a good example
Like the dog, chicken, and bear

THE SILENT WITNESS

There once was a man
Who was all alone
His face was red and pale
From where he stayed out in the cold

He had not a place to stay
But yet he always did what was right
And his life was able to glow
Even through the darkest nights

He couldn't see it but others could
As they watched him all day long
He was homeless but he was happy
And he would always listen to Gospel Songs

He never said a word but his actions did speak
As he walked along life's way
And everybody could see The Light in his life
Each and everyday

They could see Yeshua shining through his eyes
And his life reflected upon everyone there
They learned to believe and to trust in Father Yahweh
And they also learned how to care

For one day someone came
And they invited this man into their home
He never said a word but his actions did speak
For this man was nevermore alone

He could never say a word but his life was able to reflect
And he witnessed to so many souls
His life may not of been complete down here on earth
But one day it was made whole

For one day he left this world
And many tears were shed
But everybody learned that the spirit will live on
Even though the body be dead

But this man, he was always remembered
Nobody knew his name, he never did say a word
But he touched so many lives and they called him, "THE SILENT WITNESS!"
For his voice was never heard

THE TEST

Once in a person's life
They will go through a test
It's not to see who's better
Or to see who's the best

But it is a test of knowledge
And a test of wisdom too
And a test to see if you
Are able to make it through

A lot of people will fail this test
Because they do not live for Father Yahweh
But the people who pass this test
Will receive a large reward

They will live a life forever
With their Saviour up Above
Because of the life that they lived for Him
And because of their love

They will be rulers of many mansions
That Father Yahweh gave to them
And up there in Heaven
Everybody is your friend

And so if you cannot pass this test
And your soul goes astray
Then just start living your life for Father Yahweh
And you will always make an, "A!"

IN THE TWINKLE OF YOUR EYE

When I look in a person's eyes for the very first time
I can usually tell what that person is all about
Because the look in their eyes, it tells a story
And sometimes I can hear a silent shout

But when I look in a person's eyes when the sun goes down
And darkness overshadows the sky
Then I can sometimes see the reflection of a star
And I can see a twinkle in their eyes

But I wonder if that person knows the real story
That the beauty in their eyes behold
Because when I look in a person's eyes I can see
Down deep into their soul

And I can tell the real story of that person
Just by the twinkle in their eyes
I can tell if they have been hurt, heart broken, and rejected
And I can tell if they have known love in disguise

But what I can't tell is their future
For they hold their future in their hands
A lot of times people will go into water too deep
And other times they will walk into quicksand

But what is it for you my friend
I can't tell just by the twinkle in your eyes
For every twinkle has a different story
And not every twinkle comes from the sky

For some people, their twinkle, it may come from somewhere else
It don't come from the sky or from a star
And their reflection, it may not even come from a mirror
But it does come from A Far

And what I mean to say is this
That one day when you look up into the sky
There will be a Gigantic Reflection
But will The Twinkle be in your eyes

For The Reflection will be The Glory of Yeshua
And His Glory, It does Shine So Bright
But Will The Twinkle of His Glory be in your eyes
Or will you be destroyed by The Power of His Light

And so It Is something to think about
Because one day He will appear in the sky
And It can happen at just any moment
Even in the twinking of an eye

THE JOURNEY SET BEFORE ME

My life is flashing before me
And I am asking Father Yahweh what I should do
Should I journey back to where I came from
Or should I stay here with all of you

For as I sit or as I stand here
I am reminded about the day
When I left my home and set out on a journey
A journey that has made me who I am today

It was a journey unlike no other
For it helped to make me who I am
Lessons were taught and questions were answered
But they weren't taught or answered by human man

For it was the journey that helped to teach the lessons
It was the rough mountains that helped me to conquer them all
The questions were answered when I learned what it took
To get back up after a fall

Answers were given when I learned what it took
To climb up the mountain and climb back down
Lessons were taught when I learned the answers to the questions
And I learned them without hearing a sound

For the journey that was set before me
It made me stronger everyday
But the only way it could is I had to set out on that journey
And to go by faith every step of the way

For that is the answer to all of your questions
You must have faith and you must believe
You must have faith in Yeshua as He leads you on your journey
And then at the end you will achieve

You will achieve the feeling of accomplishment
Because you lived your life the way Yeshua planned it to be
Your life wasn't wasted and along the way you helped others
You helped others to see

You helped them to see the answer to all of their questions
You helped them to understand the lesson everyday
And the answer received is the same as the lesson taught
And that is to have faith in Yeshua every step of the way

5-23-2011/THE PRIVILEGED MAN

Father Yahweh laid a thought on my heart
To write on this paper today
And the thought is about the criminal on the cross
The one who said, "Remember me that day."

He said to the other criminal, "Our punishment is just.
But This Man, He has done no wrong."
But yet Yeshua suffered as He died a criminal's death
He was in the place where each of us belong

And many times I feel just like that criminal on the cross
The one who said, "Remember me that day."
For his punishment was just but yet he was privileged to die next to Yeshua
The One Who's Blood and Suffering was preparing The Way

And just as the criminal on the cross then so am I
I will never do enough good to let me in
But yet the criminal on the cross, he was very privileged
To die with Yeshua, our Truest Friend

He was privileged to die along with the one
Who was in the process of saving him, you, and me
He was privileged to die with The One Who would live again
So that all of us may be free

THE WEDDING GARMENT

When you enter into The Kingdom
What kind of clothes will you wear
Will you be wearing The Wedding Garment
Or will your clothes be full of tares

Will The King tell His servants
Chain them up and throw them away
Or will you be wearing The Wedding Garment
That allows you to stay

Is the life that you are living now
Is it full of tares
Or will your life be accepted
In The Kingdom There

Will you be a guest at The Banquet
That somehow made it in
And when The King sees you will He say,
"How did you make it in my friend?"

Will you be speechless
Because of the clothes that you where
Or will you be wearing The Wedding Garment
That says you belong there

THY SINS ARE FORGIVEN

Yeshua was in a crowded room
Teaching the people that day
When down from the roof came a paralytic man
Because coming down from the roof was the only way

Many came to hear Yeshua teach
And there was no room for the paralytic to get in
And so they got up on the roof and they lowered him down
He was lowered down by his friends

When Yeshua saw their faith He said, "Thy sins are forgiven."
"Take up thy bed and go home."
But when certain of the scribes had heard this
They reasoned in their hearts that Yeshua was wrong

But Yeshua knew what they were thinking
And so He said to them that day,
"Which is easier to say? Thy sins are forgiven
Or to take up thy bed and walk away?"

For Yeshua is The Son of Yahweh
He has The Power on earth to forgive sins
He has The Power to cause the blind to see
And to make the paralyzed mobile again

TURNING ON THE LIGHT SWITCH

Not long ago I was walking down the steps of someone's home. It had just finished raining and so when my foot hit the step I slipped and landed on my butt. When I did I realized that my smart phone was in my back pocket. When I pulled it out the screen was all shattered but to my surprise it still worked. I could make and receive phone calls, browse the internet, listen to music, and watch videos. I could still do everything that I could do before when the screen wasn't shattered. Why buy another one? It may be damaged but it still works.

The reason I share that story is because just like that broken, damaged, and shattered smart phone then so are we. When Father Yahweh looks down at us He sees us as a creature who has been damaged and He could say just like I could of said about that smart phone, "I can't use that, it's damaged," but He doesn't. When we accept Yeshua as our Saviour and our Messiah and we live for Him then Father Yahweh no longer sees that broken and shattered creature and He can use each and everyone of us if we only let Him. When we accept Yeshua then That's Who Father Yahweh sees. Yeshua stands over and in front of us and He covers the broken, the damaged, and the shattered pieces of our lives and He saves us from our sins and our sins have been washed away by and with His Blood and so when Father Yahweh looks down at us after we have accepted Yeshua as our Saviour and our Messiah and we live for Him then Father Yahweh sees Yeshua and He says, "They may be damaged but I can use him, I can use her!!!"

Science has proven that it takes 8 minutes for the light of the sun to travel and reach the earth. When we accept Yeshua as our Saviour and our Messiah it doesn't take that long for His Light to enter into us. As soon as we accept Yeshua then the cracks and shattered pieces of our lives that are filled with total darkness are immediately transformed and illuminated with The Love and The Light of Yeshua The Messiah and so when Father Yahweh saw us before we accepted Yeshua, He saw a broken, a damaged, and a shattered creature but after we accept Yeshua as our Saviour and our Messiah then when Father Yahweh looks down at us He sees Yeshua and He can use us! We might be damaged, broken, and shattered but with Yeshua in our lives Father Yahweh can use each and everyone of us!!!

I would like for everyone to look at me and if you can try to picture me with cracks and broken pieces all over my body and imagine the cracks of my life being filled with total darkness because I never accepted Yeshua as my Saviour and my Messiah.

Now picture me having accepted Yeshua as my Saviour and my Messiah and these cracks that were once filled with total darkness are now immediately transformed and illuminated with The Total Brightness of The Light and The Love of Yeshua The Messiah and that my brothers and sisters is what I believe Father Yahweh sees when He sees us after we have accepted Yeshua as our Saviour and our Messiah!!!

WALKING BY FAITH

Where were you when the lights went out
Well I was in the dark
And yes, I was a little scared
Because the wolves would howl and the dogs would bark

I admit, I was a little frightened
Because back then I didn't know
I didn't know which step to take
I didn't know where to go

Because I was afraid of making a wrong turn
I was afraid of going left instead of right
I was afraid that I would walk into a hole
And I was afraid that I would never see the light

But then all of a sudden I did take a step
And yes, I did fall into a hole
But by The Grace of Father Yahweh I got back on my feet
And that was when I asked Father Yahweh to save my soul

Because I didn't know if the next step I took
Would be my first or be my last
I didn't know if the next minute would be in my future
Or if this minute would soon be in my past

Then all of a sudden I tripped over A Book
I picked It up and It was The Book of Life
I could barely see It but One Verse said,
"Walk by faith and not by sight."

So with every step I took I learned to believe
And to trust in The One from Above
For as I was walking I stepped into several holes
But I never did fall because I was walking on The Pathway of Love

I was walking by faith and I never did fall
And I had a smile upon my face
Because trusting In Yeshua made me very happy
And I knew Yeshua was helping me make it out of this place

So I kept on walking and holding onto The Book
Holding onto The Book really tight
For Yeshua said, "My Word is A Lamp unto your feet,"
And so in darkness, It will be your Light

Then all of a sudden the darkness went away
And so I turned around so I could see
So I could see what I had accomplished by having faith in Yeshua
And I said to myself, "I'm so glad I believed!"

THE STEM OF A ROSE

The stem of a rose
Is like a limb on a tree
One blooms petals
While the other one blooms leaves

Yet each one must be cared for
Or neither one will grow
And if you come to think about it
You are like the stem of a rose

You are like the leaf on a limb
Changing all the time
Changing through different seasons
Different seasons of mankind

Seasons that you cannot predict
For everything always seems to change
Everything don't always fall into place
And sometimes life will seem strange

Because when the petals of a rose start to bloom
And the leaves on a limb turn green
And when you see things starting to change
Then you'll see exactly what I mean,

"That your life, it is like a stem.
The stem of a rose.
A rose that needs to be loved
In order for it to grow!!!"

THE REAL STORY

When a guy sees a picture of a beautiful lady
He says, "Wow! She's out of sight!"
And when a gal sees a picture of a nice looking man she says,
"I'd like to go out with him one night."

But then when you're with that person and you're not just looking at their
picture
Then your feelings about them start to change
Because you begin to see who they truly are
And that most of the time they're just out for fun and games

And then you start to see that the cover of a book
It is not the same as the pages inside
Because the pages of a book, it tells a story
The cover doesn't explain why

The cover of a book, it is just a front
The real story is what comes from within
And just because that person may look like a prince
That doesn't mean that they will be your truest friend

And so before you ever look at the cover
The part that doesn't explain why
Then open up the book and there you will see
That The Real Story is inside

TRUE BEAUTY

Beauty is so much more
Than what we see with our eyes
Just talk to an ugly person
And you may be surprised

For True Beauty is not what's on the outside
But True Beauty comes from deep within
It comes from deep within our hearts
And only from True Beauty can come True Friends

True Beauty is not an attractive look
That you see on someone's face
And True Beauty doesn't say to a beautiful person,
"Why don't you come to my place?"

But True Beauty is knowing what Love really is
True beauty is knowing how to really Love
And you can only know what Love is when you truly know Yeshua
For True Beauty is from Heaven Above

For Yeshua came from Heaven to earth
To demonstrate True Beauty for you and for me
But yet The Bible says there is no beauty in Him that we would desire Him
And so now my friends, are you starting to see

That there is a difference between beauty and True Beauty
For True Beauty is so much more than what we see
For True Beauty is The Message that comes from True Love
And True Love is The Message that Yeshua delivered, The Message
delivered to you and to me

THE WAY IT WAS MEANT TO BE

Two streams came together
Because of the direction that they flowed
Two lives came together
Because their destiny was starting to unfold

They just followed the path that was set before them
For they knew that it was the only way
They kept on believing and trusting in Father Yahweh
And believing that tomorrow would be a better day

There were times when there were hardships
And things weren't as easy as they wanted them to be
But they kept on smiling and trusting in Father Yahweh
For they believed that was their destiny

And then all of a sudden without a warning
When all of it seemed too good to be true
When all of the trials and sufferings started to make sense
And when they realized that they were going to make it through

When they passed the test that was set before them
And the trials and hardships helped to make them strong
And then afterwards when the pieces of the puzzle came together
That was when they realized that nothing was ever wrong

For all of this had led them to their destiny
For this was the way it was meant to be
For this is how the 2 streams came together
And how the man and woman were meant to be

THE POWER OF TRUE LOVE

When you see everything unfolding
Right before your very eyes
Then whatever happens next
Should be no big surprise

Because you went by faith to achieve it
And you received it with an open heart
You prayed earnestly and you asked Father Yahweh to direct you
And so now in your life a new beginning is about to start

A new beginning as a result of your decisions
And the best decision is when you took the time to pray
And the best decision also was when you decided
To put your faith in Father Yahweh every step of the way

And when you did you started noticing His Answers
You started to see everything unfold
You were amazed because all you did was go by faith
And you realized that Father Yahweh's Plans for your life are far more valuable than silver or gold

Because silver and gold cannot buy True Love
True Love is Far More Valuable than anything on this earth
And only True Love will allow you to know
The price that you are really worth

And it is not A Price that is based on worldly riches
For all of those riches will pass away
But it is A Price that is Measured by The Power of True Love
And It is only with True Love that True Friends will come your way

And then you will remember everything that had already happened
Right before your very eyes
And you will also learn that when you go by faith
Then whatever happens next should be no big surprise

WHAT WILL YOU DO WITH YESHUA

"What shall I do with Yeshua"?
Was the question that was asked that day
And the people cried, "Crucify Him!"
And so they let Barrabus walk away

The governor's wife had told him,
"Don't have anything to do with That Just Man."
But yet the people cried out all the more
And so the governor washed his hands

For the chief priest and the elders had persuaded the people
To destroy Yeshua that day
And so after the governor had washed his hands
They took Yeshua away

They spit in His Face and they beat Him
And they nailed Him to a tree
And Yeshua allowed all of this to happen
Because He Loves you and me

And so now I will ask you the question,
"What will you do with Yeshua today?"
Will you follow the crowd and say, "Crucify Him?"
And be like one of the soldiers who took Him away

Or will you be like that faithful servant
And live your life the way it is meant to be
Will you live your life completely for Yeshua
Because He loves you and me

WHY WE MUST KNOW THE BIBLE

The paper and the books may be destroyed
The pencils and ink may be no more
The Bible and Study Guides may be taken away
And there may be no one standing at the church door

For the government may take away our freedom
They may say, "If you worship Yeshua you'll be killed."
So which one of you will be the first to stand
And not be afraid of doing The Father's Will

So you better be ready and study now
Read The Bible every single day
Read and read until you know what It says
Because one day It may be taken away

They may try to take away everything that is of Yeshua
They may try to do away with Yeshua's Holy Name
And so if they do destroy and take away all of The Bibles
Then The Message of Yeshua will still be The Same

And so if we read and read and read The Bible
And we learn everything that we must know
Then even if our freedom is taken away
The Message of Yeshua will still surely show

THE WINDS OF THE SPIRIT

I was standing at a crossroads
And only one road I was allowed to choose
Which road would make me a winner
And which road would cause me to loose

Where does that road lead me
And where does that road go
Was my destiny at the end of one of these roads
I really didn't know

But yet I had no choice
For there was no other road to take
I looked to my left and then I looked to my right
And then I saw a boat upon a lake

So I walked to the boat and carefully climbed aboard
And then I took a seat when I got in
And then I folded my hands and I started to pray
And then the boat started to move with the wind

The wind would move and turn the boat
I had no control of my own
And as I was sailing I started to see
My destiny unfold

And the road I was taking wasn't even a road
But it was a boat upon a lake
And then after I climbed aboard and I started to pray
The wind blew the boat in the direction that I was meant to take

So whenever you are confused and uncertain
And you are unsure of which way to go
Then just fold your hands and start to pray
And The Winds of The Spirit will surely blow

THE REASON WE TAKE TEST

The reason that we take test
Is to determine how much we know
If we know a lot then our grade will be high
And if not, then it will be low

But in life as we take test
We usually learn as we are taking them and not before
And we don't get graded by our teachers at school
And then when the bell rings we run out the door

Because usually as we are taking this test
We are not even aware of what is at hand
Because all we are mindful of is what we are doing
Just like a drummer marching in the band

Because all they are doing is beating their drums
As they are marching in front of a crowd
And they are playing their drums with the sounds of other instruments
And the music must be played very loud

It must be played loud enough so that everyone can hear
But before the music was played to the public the band practiced everyday
And the practice to them was just like taking a test
And they became better everytime they played

And so remember in life as we are taking test
We usually learn as we are taking them and not before
Because our test in life is mainly living day by day
And trusting in Father Yahweh to lead us through the right doors

But we must be careful how we live our lives
Because a test to us may be a message to someone else you see
And the message you send could travel the earth
And it could spread for all eternity

BE GOOD TO EACH OTHER

We never know how much we really love somebody
Until they are dead and gone
So let us live the best way we can while they're alive
And never do them wrong

Because when they are dead and gone
It is too late
And we wish we could live those days again
And take back all the hate

So the days that we are allowed to live
Let us treat everybody like they are our friend
Let us be good to each other everyday
And then there will never be an end

Because the friendship that we have with somebody
Will always be here to last
And then when they are dead and gone
We will never regret the past

So let us stop saying that we hate each other
And show each other how much we care
And the reason I am writing this poem
Is because I have been there

LIVING EACH DAY AS IF IT WERE YOUR LAST

Losing someone you really love is hard
And this I know
Because several years ago
My sister had to go

My family went through a lot of pain
Because my sister, she died so young
She was out hanging around the wrong crowd
And having a lot of fun

But soon all of that fun got her into trouble
She never thought that she would leave this world
But one day she was in a car wreck
Her and this other girl

I guess it was their time to go
Or otherwise, they wouldn't have died
My sister, she was only 14
And I saw many tears being cried

But I'm not only writing this poem for me
But for a dear friend I have known for a while
Because not too long ago her father had died
And his death wiped away a lot of smiles

He was 80 years old when he died
And he was such a gentle old man
He made friends everywhere he went
And he would do anything to lend a helping hand

He would live each day as if it were his last
And he would treat everybody else the same way too
Because he knew one day he would leave this world behind
And he knew the pain that his family would be going through

He knew you didn't know what you had until it was gone
And he didn't want to leave any bad memories behind
Bad memories for his family or loved ones
And this is one of the few good men that you will ever find

So why can't we all be like this man
And live each day as if it were our last
Because not everybody has a tomorrow
But everybody does have a past

THE DIFFERENCE BETWEEN LOVE AND HOME

I never knew the difference
Between love and home
I never really understood
Until one day I was gone

I was gone away from my family
For a long, long while
And it seemed like everywhere I went
I never wore a smile

Because I could never really find
Just what I was searching for
Until that one cold night
When love came knocking at my door

And right then and there I realized
For the very first time
There is no difference between Love and Home
Because they are one of a kind

Because you put 2 and 2 together
And Home is where you hang your heart
And your heart is filled with Love
So Love at Home is where it starts

MIRACLES DO HAPPEN

It was the 16th day of June
The year was 1982
I was walking to my cousin's house
And I got hit by a car that was blue

My eyes were already set
My right leg was broken into
A man next door gave me cpr
To help me make it through

My brainstem was bruised
They said that I was gone
I was in a coma for 3 weeks
But Father Yahweh proved them wrong

I came out of my coma and I was alright
And I was in the hospital for 2 weeks more
Then they let me go home when I was better
And I rode on a wheelchair through the door

I was 5 years old when this happened
I am 37 years old now
It was 32 years ago since this happened
And people often wonder how

I will tell you how I made it
Father Yahweh performed a miracle that day
Because all of my friends and loved ones
Had got down on their knees to pray

THE DREAM OF A LIFETIME

When you are searching for the dream of a lifetime
It isn't really that hard to find
For the dream is there and so you must believe
That the doors are open all the time

And this I know for I am a dreamer
And because most of my dreams have come true
But there are many more mountains that I know I must climb
And I know that I will make it through

And so I'll just keep on climbing until I get there
And I may get some bruises if I fall
But I'll just get back up and I'll keep on climbing
And I know that I will make it through it all

And on the way I may hear some thunder
And lightning may strike the ground
Some trees may fall and some rocks may roll
But I know Where I am bound, (HEAVEN)

For my dream, it is a dream of a lifetime
And I know that this dream will come true
For my eyes are focused and I'm doing what is right
And I know what I must do

I must keep on dreaming and I must still believe,
That the doors are open all the time
And then when I get to the end of the road I will achieve
The dream that I long to find

Because the doors that I ask for, they are already open
And so it is up to me to believe and walk through
And this I know for I am a dreamer
And because most of my dreams have already come true

This is a poem of faith. We must always believe and trust in Father Yahweh and Yeshua and no matter how hard the road may seem to be we must accept it and still believe because it is part of our destiny because on this road we will learn strength and sharpen our character. All of the doors that we ask Father Yahweh to open are already open if they are in accordance to Father Yahweh's Will in our life and so we must go by faith, no matter what we are going through, and we will walk through those doors!!!

RICH MAN AND POOR MAN

The life of a rich man is a dream
That everyone has in their soul
Because of all the wealth and money
And everything else that goes

The life of a poor man is a life
That no one wants to live
Because everybody thinks that the poor man
Don't have anything to give

But if the rich man don't have love
And the poor man does
Then the rich man is not as rich
As he thought he was

The poor man is more rich
Because he is happier inside
And the rich man is poor
Because in his heart he has too much pride

He thinks that he can buy his love
He thinks that money is the answer to everything
But what the rich man don't realize is
He don't have anything unless he has a dream

And the dream of a rich man is to be loved
That is the biggest dream in the world
And then he will see the difference between money and love
Is that love is the bigger reward

So if the rich man don't have love
And the poor man does
Then the rich man is not as rich
As he thought he was

RACISM

A lot of people in this world today
Have something against a different race
It does not matter if you are black or white
So let us make this world a better place

Because black or white, we are all the same
Just a different color of skin
Let us not hate people because of their color
Let's just be each other's friend

Let us put a stop to all of this prejudice
And put a stop to all of this hate
Let us make this world a better place
Especially for our children's sake

Because our children will learn as they live
And they will do a lot of what they see
So let us put a stop to all of this hatred
And let us be the best that we can be

Because having hatred in our hearts
Will get us no where in life
But if we be good to each other all of the time
Then there will not be any trouble and strife

So let us not have any hatred in our hearts
Let's just be each other's friend
Then this world will be a better place
For every color of skin

THE ONE GIFT THAT WE ALL HAVE GOT

Everyone has a gift
What they do with it is up to them
But the most important gift that we all have got
Is the gift of being someone's friend

So don't go around thinking that you are better than someone
Because deep inside you are not
You may just believe in yourself a little bit more
But there is one thing that we all have got

We have all got a gift and the ability to do something
But The Strength must come from Yeshua, our Truest Friend
And this I know because I have been there
And let me just tell you one more thing my friend

Sometimes the road will seem long and endless
And sometimes the days will seem like nights
But then when you get to the end of the road you will have made it
And I promise, you will see The Light

And you will see that we all have a gift
And That The Strength must come from Yeshua, our Truest Friend
And you will see that the one gift that we all have got
Is the gift of being someone's friend

THE INTERNATIONAL LANGUAGE

In the beginning of time there was one language
There was one woman, there was one man
But Father Yahweh said, "Be fruitful and multiply."
And so mankind started to expand

Mankind started to grow
And they became smarter everyday
But something had to happen
To make man go their separate ways

For you see there was a group of people
Who tried to build a tower beyond the sky
Right after Father Yahweh told them not to
But He never asked them why

He never asked them, "Why didn't you listen?"
He just confused their language that day
And so that is what had to happen
To make man go their separate ways

For man could not understand one another
And so they had to go
They had to go to where they were comfortable
And to a language that they did know

And so that is why there is many languages
In this world today
Because instead of listening to Father Yahweh
Man chose another way

But yet there is still one thing
That will always be
There is one thing in all of our languages
That we will always see

Even though we all may speak a different language
And we all may have a different name
There is still one thing in all of our languages
That we will always speak the same

Even though we may never be able to understand one another
And we may never be able to ask each other why
One thing in all of our languages that we will always speak the same
Is a laugh and a cry

ANGELS IN DISGUISE

The idea of this poem had popped in my mind
Just the other day
I was thinking of the words to write for this poem
But I didn't know what to say

I thought all day and I thought all night
But then I got tired and so I went to bed
I couldn't sleep and so I got up
And then the words just kept popping in my head

It was unbelievable, I couldn't believe it
As the words kept draining from the pen
And as the words fell on the paper I began to understand
The message that I'm to send

And the message I am sending is look beside you
Look around you everyday
There is always someone who needs a friend
And help along the way

And there is always someone whom you may not see
That is an angel in disguise
They are always there but you will never see them
Just by looking through your eyes

You have to feel it with your heart and read it with your mind
And then put the two together so you can see
That an angel in disguise, it can be any person
It can be you or me

For I remember many of times when I helped a stranger
I helped an old man carry his groceries one day
He had tears in his eyes and to him I was an angel
For I had helped him along the way

And there's been many a times when a stranger has helped me
They gave me clothes and a warm place to sleep
They gave me a job when I needed money
And they gave me plenty of food to eat

Now most of these people I have only seen one time
And you know, I may never see them again
But there's one thing for sure, there's one thing I've learned
We're all capable of being each other's friend

And so the message has to get out across the country
It has to get out from sea to shining sea
It's time to let all people know and it's time to show
That an angel can be you or me

And now look at the person who is talking to you
Can you tell, can you see
Can you tell if they're an angel in disguise just by looking through your eyes
And if you can, then please tell me

HOW NOT TO FORGET YOUR ANNIVERSARY

When I get married I think I should marry a lady
Whose birthday is the same day as mine
That way when her birthday comes I should not forget it
And then her birthday present should be right on time

When we get married I think we should get married on her birthday
Because after all our birthdays will be the same
And that way when our birthday comes I will know it's our anniversary
Because they will fall on the same day

But what should happen if I forget my birthday
Then I would absolutely forget her birthday too
And if I forgot our birthday would I forget our anniversary
And if I did, what would she do

Would she get mad or would she still love me
Would she forget or remember the day
Well here is my plan and I will not forget it
I am going to love her every step of the way

And so if I happen to forget our birthday and anniversary
But yet I remember to love her with all of my might
Then she should never get mad if I ever forget
Because the love that we'll have will be out of sight

GIFT OF LIFE

The gift of life is a newborn baby
A special gift shared by 2
By 2 people who really love each other
And want to share the rest of their lives through

And share their lives with their baby
Whether it be a little boy or girl
Because after all it is a special gift
That was brought into this world

Another life to keep you going on
And to give you another reason to live
Because now you have someone that you can call your own
And you know to your baby you will give

You will give to your baby a special life
And you will raise your baby to do what is right
Because one day your baby will grow up
And he or she will see the light

Because one day they will be a parent
And they will bring a special gift into this world
And they are going to love that baby no matter what
Whether it be a little boy or girl

IN ONLY A DAY

If I were rich for a day
And as strong and as fast as I wanted to be
I think I would buy me a shovel
And do something that all the world would see

I would dig down to the bottom of the earth
And then I would get beneath the 3rd rock from the sun
I would gently pick it up
And then I would run

I would run and take the earth up to Heaven
I would take the bad with the good
And since no evil is allowed in Heaven
Then all would be like it should

The bad will be separated from the good
The tares will be separated from the wheat
And then no more sin will be on the earth
And then everything will be so sweet

I will then run and take the earth back down
And it will once again be the 3rd rock from the sun
And then after I gently lay it down
I will say, "That was fun!"

I will then run and get back upon the earth
And I will hire some helping hands
And we will buy enough Bibles and hand Them All out
To every child, woman, and man

We will buy food for all of the hungry
And houses for those without
And where ever there is a need it will be met
Because that is what it's all about

I will then pay all of those who helped me
And then I will give the rest of my money away
And then I will fall on my knees in amazement
Because all of this happened in only a day

I will then run back home and go to bed
Because I will probably be tired and want to sleep
And then as I am sleeping I want to dream
Of Yeshua taking care of His sheep

And then when I wake up the next day
And I am not as strong or as fast as the day before
I will still wear a smile on my face
As I walk out the door

For I'll know down deep in my heart
That I am richer now than I could ever be
Even though I'm not as strong or as fast
And I don't have any money

For I was very rich in money for only a day
I was very fast and very strong
But Yeshua through me, He met every need
And He made right where there was wrong

And now everybody on the earth is very happy
Everybody has a home and plenty of food to eat
And everybody now knows Yeshua
And they all shall worship Him at His Feet

And now earth is like Paradise
It is like Heaven in a way
Because everybody is happy and Praising Yeshua
And all of this happened in only a day

VISIONS OF VICTORY

One night as I was sleeping
I had an awesome dream
I dreamed that I was on top of a cloud
And I could see so many things

I could see knights in shining armor
Marching off into the day
And then I looked around and I saw Some Children
On the other side of the bay

And then I looked and I saw a young lady
She was only about 14
And this young lady, she had a vision
She had a Vision of a Beam

The Vision was a Beam of Light
And It was so Radiant to her eyes
She jumped on her feet and she followed It
And this is what was to her surprise

That where the Beam of Light stood still
That's where she found An Awesome Book
She picked it up, then looked towards Heaven
And then she looked back down and took a look

She flipped through The Chapters of This Awesome Book
And then she saw in Fine Red Print,
"I COME QUICKLY!" and then she looked up
From Where The Beam of Light was sent

And then she laid The Book wide open
Wide open on the ground
And then The Beam of Light stood over The Red Print
And It made An Awesome Sound

And The Sound It made was Unexplainable
For It was The Most Beautiful Thing that I had ever heard
And everyone there, they knew
The incident that occurred

For The Voice said, "I COME QUICKLY!"
And everyone ran to where The Awesome Book lay
And they all got down and repented
For they knew Yeshua was on His Way

And then the little girl, she did come quickly
And to my amazement she stepped on The Book
And then The Beam of Light expanded all the way through the sky
And everyone there did look

For the little girl shot up through The Beam
And she came straight up into the sky
And as she came up she had a smile on her face
She waved at me and said, "Hi."

And then I looked back down and I saw the knights in shining armor
And they just came marching on in
They were going to kill the people who saw The Vision
For they knew it was nearing the end

The knights didn't want The Word to be spread
Then all of a sudden The Children came charging through
They tore down the knights with just The Power of Their Speed
And then the people who witnessed it, they came up too

Now the knights in shining armor were angels from the dark side
The Children were Angels of Light
The little girl, well, she was just a person
Who by faith delivered a message that night

The Awesome Book is The Word of Father Yahweh
The Beam of Light was The Holy Spirit from Above
The Fine Red Print is The Words of Yeshua
Words filled with So Much Love

The Awesome Sound was The Voice of Father Yahweh
The Beam of Light is What carried The Voice out
The people were those who were faithful to Father Yahweh
And they knew what It was all about

The Power of Their Speed is The Power of Father Yahweh
That knocked all of the knights down
And as I was looking I saw
All of the knights laying dead on the ground

And I am just simply a person
Who beheld a Beautiful Sight
For I had VISIONS OF VICTORY
As I dreamed I was on a cloud one night

THE GOOD SHEPHERD

Why did The Angels go to the shepherds
The night that Mary gave birth
The night she gave birth to Yeshua, The Redeemer of the world
And The Savior of planet earth

Why didn't The Angels go to a king or a ruler
Of a nation or of a kingdom that night
Why did The Angels go to the Shepherds while they were watching their sheep
And tell them about This Marvelous Sight

And why was Yeshua born in a manger
And not in a mansion on top of a hill
Why were all of the rooms full at the motel that night
Was this all part of Father Yahweh's Perfect Will

Well I believe that the answer is, "Yes."
It was meant for The Messiah to be born in a manger that night
And I also believe that it was meant for The Angels
To tell the shepherds about This Marvelous Sight

And so since The Messiah was born in a manger
And not in a mansion on top of a hill
And since The Angels went to the shepherds while they were watching their sheep
Then it sounds just like Father Yahweh's Perfect Will

For Yeshua did not come as someone born rich
He was born in a manger with animals and hay
He was born to be our Shepherd and to be The Keeper of His sheep
So that none of us should go astray

And so The Reason that I believe that The Angels went to
The shepherds while they were watching their sheep
Is because Yeshua is our Shepherd and we are His sheep
And Yeshua never sleeps

For Yeshua is The Good Shepherd
And He takes care of us all
He walks with us everyday
And He helps us up each time we fall

Yes, Yeshua is The Good Shepherd
And we are His sheep
We are the sheep of His Pasture
And He is The Shepherd Who never sleeps

Printed in the United States
By Bookmasters